PREVIOUSLY
FEARED
DARKNESS

PREVIOUSLY

FEARED

DARKNESS

POEMS

ROBERT

PRIEST

ECW
PRESS
MISFIT

COPYRIGHT
©
ROBERT PRIEST
2013

Published by ECW Press
2120 Queen Street East, Suite 200, Toronto, Ontario, Canada M4E 1E2
416-694-3348 / info@ecwpress.com

Library and Archives Canada Cataloguing in Publication

Priest, Robert, 1951–, author
Previously feared darkness : poems / Robert Priest.

ISBN 978-1-77041-164-7 (PBK)
ALSO ISSUED AS: 978-1-77090-447-7 (PDF) / 978-1-77090-448-4 (ePUB)

I. Title.

PS8581.R47P74 2013   C811'.54   C2013-902488-3

Editor for the press: Michael Holmes / a misFit book
Cover and text design: Natalie Olsen, Kisscut Design
Printed and bound in Canada by Coach House   5 4 3 2 1

The publication of *Previously Feared Darkness* has been generously supported by the Canada Council for the Arts which last year invested $157 million to bring the arts to Canadians throughout the country, and by the Ontario Arts Council, an agency of the Government of Ontario. We also acknowledge the financial support of the Government of Canada through the Canada Book Fund for our publishing activities, and the contribution of the Government of Ontario through the Ontario Book Publishing Tax Credit and the Ontario Media Development Corporation.

Purchase the print edition and receive the eBook free!
For details, go to ecwpress.com/eBook.

Dedicated to
my beloved Marsha Kirzner

This book remembers Harold and
Mildred Kirzner, Uncle Jimmy Finan,
Phil and Jenny Klotz, Helen Kirzner,
Alan Mador, Shirley Vernon, Arlene
Mantle, Jack Layton, Peter Kormos,
Elijah Harper, Aniko Zend, and
Henry Morgentaler

CONTENTS

And Poetry Started to Rush Out

A hole opened in the sky
And poetry started to rush out

At first we thought there must be so much poetry
It would take forever to empty the world

But each poem stretched the hole wider
And so now we must get to work again

We must breathe into the word
And let language rise up among us

If there is no poetry left in the world
Our kind will die forever

Without poetry we will not walk
Into the middle of the river

Just to see what's done
To our reflections by the waves

Quicker than time can drag poetry
Gasping away forever

We must make up the new world
New words new ways

All the Information in the Sun

All the information in the sun
Cannot disappear forever

From the universe
Deny light all you like

The dark data shows up anyway
Under your lids

Under your feet
In the part of your palm

You can't read
You can't know enough

Dark data to predict
Its effect on any future

Matter
The road may or may not be there

At the next step
The journey may go on

Whether or not you disappear
Into the distance

Nothing Came

Nothing came
Though waiting had happened

Nothing came
On the 4 a.m. bus

Out of nowhere
We waited and we waited some more

But nothing came
Nothing came to nothing

And so we sat with that
Like arrival

Till it was a place
Or a being

In fact it was us
This locus of nothing

And it hurt like hell
Nothingness in us

Tugging at us
Wanting to be something

If we go on waiting I believe
The bus will arrive

And we will once again
Have nothing in our arms

It's Not the Moon That Is Mad

It's not the moon that is mad
It's the sea inside the head

Of that sad man imagining the end
Water is not evil

But it is evil to leave the water
Dying or dead

It is not the stars that are enraged
It is not the sky that seethes with murder

It is that man walking down the long road
It is the blossom inside his mind

The ultimate rose rich and red
The man is afraid

But it is not the man
Who should be afraid

Portrait of a Harper

How soothingly he strums and plucks
He knows the song you want to hear

Not given much to melody
But economic soporific

The notes he plays are rarely wrong
Barely a hint of the real song

Running through his mind
Cutting through his smile

He just plucks you lullabies
And does his best to meet your eyes

He is but an instrument himself he says
Yes, what a harp, what a lyre this harper is

Making It Wait

He skates on the skin of his teeth
A razor-thin grin
Cut into a Gumby mask
Nothing he does can make it look real
He can't help but suggest
An eraser

In a cartoon
He would be the trickster
Who comes in and rubs
Stuff out
The trick is to tickle him into a grin
Or trigger a photo op
Make him reveal
His Achilles smile

He wants to rub out words
He wants to rub out agreements
But he has to go through the machinery
Of state
Lately he's had to resort to merely making things wait
But then he sees the virtue in it
Yes to stalling
He prorogues parliament
Once, twice
Just a little bit of delay
Who has waited more?
It's a way of rubbing something out
Very very slowly
One day he'll really hit the brakes
But for now on that icy grin
He skates
And waits

A Streetcar Named Delay

Standing round a ringed red pole
Spending quantity time
With people we don't know
We're in wait training
Me, Godot, the ferryman, the messiah — the whole crowd
In a holding pattern

Feel the waiting, people
Waiting is good for the economy
So says the mayor
The waiting skills we acquire now will serve us later
When we wait for jobs, for operations, for painkillers

Few of us step out repeatedly
Into the middle of the road
To stare along the chock-a-block car tops
For some distant curve of coach at the event horizon
But look! What bus, its hour come at last, slouches toward us to be —
No! The words "Out of service" become legible
No! The driver creeps by beaming
But absolutely no one curses
No one pounds a fist in rage
Our breath mists may mingle in the darkening night air
But if our eyes meet
It is only to shake our heads and shrug that
We didn't walk home when we had the chance
We could have been in the warm and dry right now
But we are still here at the all-you-can-wait
Absorbing stasis and delay and frost
Sucking up the longing, miles and miles of deeply embodied longing

We are not alone
All across the city taut elastic tightens in the chest
A protracted hope stretched thin
That one day like a kind of lateral rapture
Our car will come
And we will herd on into the herd
Squeeze in among the squeezed
And it will at last lurch forward
At least half a block
Before
It hits gridlock
And stops
And jerks forward again
And hits gridlock
And stops
And stops
And stops

Definitions and Titles

Pooration: 1. the process of making a populace poor
             2. pooration to the point where cuts are made to
                the core essentials of life is
                known as *core pooration.*
             See also: *povertization* and *topple down economics*
             See also: *prausterity*

The Waistland

We are the stuffed men
All circumference
All diameter
Obese-city
Omni-grazers
Swelling on the fat
Of the land
Where belt is the new infinity
Where every day we increase our waist
And our waist is in your face
It's in common view our waist spills over
And flops itself into the scoff and gobble of culture
And there's pills to make you want to stop eating
And all the food is dreadful
And we've lost our navels
And we can't reach round to our own flopsy genitals
And our hearts are so fat
No two fishermen
Can sit side by side on any one dock
And no two CEOs
Can share any one limousine
And there are fat arses
Bigger than the backs of buses
Bursting with vile gases
And there are new waists about the wrists
And a wave of waists in the underneck
I have waists and waists and waists
Thickening in my face
We are people of glut
We split the seams of the world's

Boxers
With immeasurable
Excess
Quivering acres of jellied "us"
So liquid
They can never be assessed

This is the way the word ends
This is the way the word ends
This is the way the word ends
Not with a bang
But hemorrhoids

Asshole Sky

It's an asshole sky
Too tight for oblivion
Blind in one eye
Stuffed with the divine
Rectitude
The sky is fucking bovine
It whines like an ox
Grey with attrition
Someone sucked the sky stupid
And it got soft and dissolute
It can't hold its stool
The sky is an old man in a home
Too stooped to poop
We are infinity's nurse
Urging the worst of it out
Dirty as Job
We pull faith from the rabbit's
Asshole hat
Ears first toes kicking
Look at that
The sky's child
Wriggling raw
With its first cry
I, aye
It's a shite sky
A maggot moon
It's skin pore heaven up there
An opening bigger than Jupiter
Infinitely wide
But rotten inside
It's a mammoth going off to die
A dead star with a blinded eye

It's an asshole sky

Aztechs

Aztech drones hone the knife in the sky

Obsidian missiles
Plunge into the ribs of the world

Pulling out an infant heart
And eating it, still beating

Aztech jets
High over the next people
And the next

Tezcatlipoca smiles

Ah here's Saddam, his chest
Excavated
He's thrown down the steps
Before his people
His death made sacred
By a hundred thousand
Million
Previous deaths
Here's Khaddafi
Rifle-raped
Here's the collateral babes of Homs
Bent backwards over the pyramid tops

Ask the Aztech jets
Is the great Quetzalcoatl satisfied yet?
Have the people paid their debt?

Not yet not yet

Lennon

The sky was a blue throat with no scream
And then came Lennon raw with rage

There were no tears on earth
And Lennon was the salt and the rain

He bittered the air with his lament
And dared in the end utter hope

Then Lennon left
The songs blown from his chest

Beyond his soul
A split widening the sky

Where the world
Got bigger than the world

Could hold

Lennon Backwards by Bed

I

She lies back flat on the bed
Fully dressed
Her gaze, her arms away from him
He's naked on his side, pressed against her
One long leg, bent across her chest
His arm and wrist
Framing and holding her face

Just as his lips touch her cheek
Annie Leibovitz clicks
It's voted the world's all-time #1 magazine cover
It's his last morning on earth

II

Their peace ad and honeymoon
Bed-in bed
Where journalists
Lie down with them
For interviews
The bed they share with her daughter
With celebrities
And TV crews
Selling non-violence like soap

From this bed he sings
"Give Peace a Chance"
In a great raw holler
And it's a worldwide hit

III

A very Jesus-looking man rolls a hospital bed
Into Abbey Road Studios
His lover in it recovering from a car crash
"We can't bear to be apart,"
He tells the other Beatles
They're annoyed but go ahead
Their final album recorded in the presence of this bed

IV

After a gig
Two motherless men
Enter a hotel room

Face to face
On the ends of twin beds,
A lefty and a righty
They finish off their first American number one
"She Loves You"
To synchronize the harmonies
They lean in close
And watch each other's lips

V

"Out of this rock"
 Is the motto of the school
 The schoolboy hates
 He'd rather lie in bed all day and float upstream
 Aunt Mimi calls him lazy
 An underachiever
 But he knows already he's got something
 Though he's never even heard of rock and roll

VI

Age three, his mother
Lets him sleep with her
In the same bed as her lover
Aunt Mimi reports them
Aunt Mimi steals him from that bed
To which he can never find his way back

VII

1942
Incendiaries fall on Liverpool all night long
The worst raid of the war and newborn John
For safety's sake
Is placed beneath the bed
Beneath the bed his first night on earth Lennon screams
That great raw holler in fine form
as the bombs roar

Acorn's Oak

There should be some kind of oak
And great oak boughs above
The place where Acorn broke the law
When he shouted I shout love
In Allan Gardens week after week
Where Acorn spoke
There should be some kind of oak

There by the bust of Robbie Burns
Where Acorn roared
Through streams of reeking cigar smoke
That tree should be deep-rooted, firm
Enough to hold this place of poetry
And mark the time and the law he broke
By speaking in a public park
To all the crowds of Sunday folk
Who came to Allan Gardens
Week after week
To hear him speak

There should be some kind of oak
And great oak boughs above
The place where Acorn disobeyed
When he shouted I shout love

The Leonard Koans

Let us compare dictionaries
What happens when

An infinitely moving melody
Meets an utterly implacable voice?

There is a melody
With no notes at all

It is so we may travel with her
That we are blind

We are all connected by
One blue butterfly

You may even take away
What is there for good

If you take away
A poet's money —

Go buy rivers
Buy yard goods

In my secret life
I shout his praises, I sing his songs

I bellow them
If there's a way to say goodbye don't

When a Leonard Cohen song ends
It is not over

Jinx

Einstein and Heidelberg both said
"There's no simultaneity
over vast distances"
at exactly the same time

Give Us a Floor

Give us a floor we can drag a chair over
And leave a mark
A hardwood floor that can take a lot of dancing
We want a floor that you leave your shoes on and tap when you like
A floor you can jump on
Give us a floor where a kid can bang a hammer for an hour
And no one cares
We want a good flat floor strong enough for a piano or two
A floor that can bear the weight of ten bass amps
Fifty stomping bikers on choppers
And still be fine for yoga in the morning
It is important to have a floor you can fall on
A floor good for trying risky positions
Tipsy calisthenics
Maybe one day we'll want to invite
Multi-faith obesity groups intent on leaping and praying
A floor equipped to bear them all
And still take a child's lightest footfall
With never the creak of any small floor complaint
A floor to hold up the elephants
And hippopotami
A floor, please, to take the great weight of human hearts
Held in thrall by mere matter
By love by stampede
We want a floor to bear seven generations
Each unfolded out of the other
All at once in a great hootenanny and holler
A floor to bear the greatest table ever made
For a feast where no one's missing
We don't want some poor flat excuse

We don't want some bottom-line trapdoor
We want a floor to hold the world up when it's exhausted
A floor to keep the sky on when it's drained and dry
And ready to fall

It's time we had the floor
Give us the floor

Rights Left

(Marching song)

Rights left
Rights left
We still have some
rights left
right?

Left? Right! Left? Right!
(Left right left right)
We still have some
(left right) left —
Right?

Quick march!

I was just enquiring about
the rights left

Rights left?

Yes, the rights left to us by our ancestors
The rights left to our children and their children
The right to free speech
That's left, right?
The right to freedom of assembly
That's left, right?
The right to collective bargaining
That's left, right?
We have rights left to gain
not rights left to lose
We have rights left to fight for
We must increase the number of rights left, right?

What if we left right
at the moment someone was trying to reduce
the number of rights left?
Pretty soon nothing would be left, right?

Left? Right?
Right?

We Are Not Dammed

We are not dammed
Not by our blood
Not by our flesh
We flow around such obstacles
We seep through
We simply evaporate
And return
Nor can our sins dam us
We are rivers that perpetually break their bonds
Ice cannot block us
We are not dammed by being compact
By being bone
We are not dammed by block-headedness
Nothing can hold us back forever
We are not stopped
Locked
Not even by god for good
Suddenly we cut loose
Go with the flow
Let the blessing erode
The curse
Let the flood come
And the banks burst
And the spirit in us
Grow in common current
Unrehearsed unpredictable
A risky wave to lift the earth
Up to the sky like a bubble
On a surge
And in real-time wind
Let it go

One Day I Predict

One day I predict
We'll be amazed
At our strength
We will look at one another
Astonished and say
We didn't think we could do this

One day the path will be so clear
We will all say: it's obvious
And we will hardly believe
We couldn't see the way before

One day I predict
We'll have this great true story to tell
A kind of anti-*Iliad*
For the coming age
Involving all of us
Who think we are not warriors
And all of us who fear
We are not brave

The New Slogans

Homophobia is a choice

•

Love and let love

•

Vaginal birth not virginal birth

•

If the well is well the people are well as well

•

Stop global warring

•

It takes the whole world to make one peace

•

Only conscience is consciousness

•

Peace won't make itself

•

Homes not drones!

•

You never know where a good thing is gonna come from

•

New clear news! New clear information! New clear action!

•

We are all slightly indivisible

•

Resistance is fertile

Poem for Trumpet

Blow ragged horn of bone
Leave a red ring round my mouth
Blow harsh horn
Of human tragedy
Horn carved from a man's leg
Blow flesh trumpet
Take this compressed ring
Of sorrow from the chest's hollow
Cry meat horn in red raw blare
Let out the burn
The fraying
I give you a brass version of grief
I give you trivalved sorrow
Slurring down
Harried scales of funk
Half drunk
On its own bleak tone
O trumpet drain my inertia
Make golden my anger
Lift up my life in
Double-tongued runs
Make me even with heaven
And don't let go
Till I let go
My embouchure blown
But playing on anyway
Breath hissing from the sides
Of my mouth
My lips numb rubbery but
The silver still coming at me

Little flakes of tone flying off
Like a throat hoarse from crying
But crying on anyway
Reedlike rupturing
Every rasp necessary
To the absolution of this
Particular bout
Of the blues
The true final note
Being the long drained silence
That ensues

V

When Churchill flashed his famous V sign
It wasn't for victory
As everyone says
It was for vagina
For he knew
What I know
That there is still not enough praise
For the vagina
He knew that if anything is miraculous
The relation between the inside of the vagina
And the outside of the penis
Is

Nixon knew it too
Even as he resigned
Even as he turned to face the music
Of his own destiny
He flashed that last V
But my friends
It was not a sign of peace
It was Nixon's way of saying
That the inside of the vagina
Is as numinous as it gets

This secret is well known
The vagina is a sign
Without which not a single holy thing
May be written

Two Million and One (I Love You All)

I love you all
Which would be okay if I didn't have a "double standard"
But I want all of you to be faithful to me
I will go mad if any of you betray me
We are as though married in my mind
We have an everlasting spiritual bond
It's something about your faces
I want each of you so badly
I am a hurricane of blushing
I want you in my bed, in my blood
I want to have your children, meet your mothers
I want to spend sacred days with each of you
Let you tempt up from silence my poor little whining silences
And nurture them into poetry, song, brags, raps, and rants
Yes, I may need some longevity for this
I may need some income and perhaps a change of the law
But I will know each of you intimately
Intuitive about your deepest, least spoken needs
Hip to your doubts, your talents, your fault lines
I want to know the tastes of your mouths
The distinct curves of each and every
Breast, buttock, cheekbone
It is as though we met in other lives
I feel your full-force love coming back too
I feel your divine intent at me
I feel the compass tug awhirl in two million hearts to me
And me to you to you and to you
I even want to go through the bad bits with all of you
What it is you want in bed
What you say on bleak mornings

When your look is the poke of a long cold pole at the soul
And I will swear two million oaths if I must
If each of you say: Yes
I will keep lawyers employed
I will build a city upon pre-nups
What vats of oils for libations we shall pour upon each other
In the merrymaking we shall have
What vapours our two million and one sighs shall make
A veritable weather system of sighs

Between Your Disconnection and Mine

between your disconnection
and mine

that other
united states

we have been kept
apart by Canada

which is what?
a series of provinces

I will not let Alberta
stand between us

I will take a train
I will see the sea

I've melted all my ingots
in the sun of your stare

I've cracked the last diamond
to the finest tiny diamond inside

and even at the tip of my tongue
I felt that tinier tip yet

the as yet undiscovered bit
of the tongue

you need to say "love" precisely
love, love, concision has made me strange

I cut corners in words
I should have found you by now

everything points toward you
the very land leads down

we'll wind up in
the same gullies

no matter what
we say

we'll be at the crest
of the same waves

still not making
eye contact

I will stand with you
at the very feet of god

and neither you nor I
will finally nod

or what?
we could break

all the great spells
of time and circumstance

with a glance

Raw (Like You Like It)

Nothing between you
And the universe

Raw like you like it
Part of you is part of it

All the rest rests
Mutually between

Yang and yin
Nothing not you

And her / him
Raw like you like it

Miracle

Whoever made up the word
Miracle
Was wrong

We have been touched
By the ordinary

We have been altered
By the immutable

Whoever made up the word
Love
Was right

A genius

It is perfect

It Smells More Like a Rose
(Than the Rose Itself)

It smells more like a rose
Than the rose itself

The vertical grin

Like having two big dots
On the bottom of the exclamation mark

The *V* bent over
The bottom of the bed
Wide open

All capital *I*'s aslant
Slightly fatter

Texty texty stuff
Typo-erotic

Whether pressed into flesh
Wax or the fovea centralis

Of the widening eye
A sign the size of the world

A word
Bigger than the whole language

Stopped, stuttering
Trying to get out of you

The Tongue

The tongue has no bone
But look how mobile it is
Without so much as a joint it can curve back on itself
It can double under
The tongue can form a tight *V* at the tip
The tongue can run its stuff roughshod up the sucker's back
Or solicit triplets tenderly from a trumpet in synchronized breaths
All of this and it tastes too
So close to mind
It seems almost a part of mind
Its movements those of thought
Instinct
It darts it probes
When we kiss and share tongues
We trade inputs
It's the pleasure of mind to mind
The tongue tasting the tongue
The tongue that titillates
With tipsy precision
The tongue tipped sideways into crevices seeking out bits and pieces
Cracks and seeds
A tongue able to thrust itself forward far beyond the perimeter
The tongue so powerful
It can pierce the heart of a ripe peach
And tear away the flesh without need of teeth

Miniatures

I can count the universe on one finger

•

Don't catch the sharp side

•

One vine climbs another

•

The sun is a thought too bright to look at

•

The sky is completely unedited

•

The sun is wireless

•

The only thing holding up the trellis is the morning glories

•

I have openings for tomorrow
A yellow one which is a flower
A blue one — the sky
And two with lashes
My eyes

•

Love is not the answer
It is the question

It is the command

Our Wounds

They can't heal for us going at them in our sleep
Secretly opening them again

Like Penelope
We replay our wounds

Unwind our wounds
And weave our wounds again

But our wounds have no nutrition
Our wounds unravel us

Into and through
Every opening opening a smaller and smaller opening

Our tongues as we sing and salivate
Sharper ever sharper

Rotator Cuff

My shoulder is a chip on itself
It is one side of a wave reared up against my head, my hairdo
Both are extensions of my shoulder
I am still hunched to the rifle
Hump to the shovel
I have shoulders to keep the hat above my ears
And on my left shoulder the cannon
And on my right the dove
My shoulder is a mountain in the making
Ragged pulleys pickaxes chip away at it
My shoulder is a glacier retreating
An ice floe tipping into the north wind
One side of a star tacked up to a hockey stick
My shoulder swivels like a target
It hangs like a ragged sock
Some frightened animal is trying to get out of my shoulder
And every movement beats its fibre with a bat
My shoulder is a failed epaulette hung in tatters
From the gallows pole
It rips at itself like a bird with one wing
Every string taut and tugged
A snowbank on a one-way highway
It is a butchered moose
Roadkill on a rack
Something on the end of it
Flapping in the sky
A hand
Trying to write

Industrial Accident 3

Time revved its wheels at the back base of my thumb
At the bottom back of my index finger
In that *V* there
My skin was stripped out
Burned bare

I saw the grid coming through my hand
I saw the latticework underneath the crisscrosses
I still feel the scaffold in it always

My hand where a burning god walked
Where gears of skin meshed
Standing up now without a staff
Having woven new flesh from old
Having knit new nerves from old
It extracts from broken glass
New clear panes

Once crushed in the tons of machine
It now pulls from thread
The delicate thread
Within the thread

False Memory Syndrome 1

I woke up and I was four and I was alone in a house painted red
And I reached the red chair and climbed up to the red cupboard
Where there was a bottle of red
And red was everywhere and everything
Red you hate like god
Red you despise like life
Red as the love you left lying
The love you left dying
Red as a bluebell, red as moon water
And I looked up and the stars were red and the leaves were red
And I screamed red air into the room

My Thought

my thought is raw a river without reflection its top surface gone
my thought is skinless as much a part of body as being it plucks
me like a finger plucks a violin it spirals down a corkscrew
ever on turn turn my thought sinks in muck it drowns in toxic
bogs goes round in thought-mills repeating shit my thought
on automatic like ticker tape my thought sucks like a drunk on
the body's dry bottle it gnaws at the pineal gland like its own
personal charm it paws my times like a glutton with only one
bead it worries me it snaps back it unravels and you see the
severed threads in my eyes there are de-tuned sinews skewing
my senses the world is coming in like the sea through nets my
thought flies it runs it leaps through knots a grid a lyre always
cutting the nexus a new crisscross tipping me over still kicking
into the abyss a motor of string unravelling in free fall always
knitting itself a new one

Book of Jobs

Once God was talking to Satan and He commented how pleased He was now that people were finally good. Now that they finally truly loved Him. But Satan said, "They love you because you have given them abundant lives and much freedom. It's not yourself they love you for." In this way God was tricked into testing people. To settle the issue with Satan he destroyed all unions everywhere. Even without their unions most people clearly still loved God. But Satan was unconvinced. So God took away safety regulations and then he took away health care and many of them were burned or had their hands crushed but still the great masses of people continued loving God. Satan was not persuaded. "They still have jobs. They still have purpose. That is what they love," he asserted. Ten million jobs disappeared with a wave of God's hand but Satan just sneered. So God took away their social assistance and then their employment insurance. When love of God remained high it was clear that Satan was beginning to waver. But God went even further to make his point. He took away their homes. He took away their rights. He even took away their family bonds so that they fell to fighting among each other. "Do you see how human love for God is undiminished?" he gloated. "Look!" he roared. He began to kill their children. They were crushed by cars. They were blown up by roadside bombs. They fell into fratricidal wars and a great hunger fell over all the earth. But even more frequently the people fell to their knees and prayed. Even more loudly they yelled their devotions.

iSlam Cancelled!

Due to unforeseen legal difficulties this year's iSlam has been cancelled. Ticket holders are strongly advised not to proceed to the event under any circumstances. Messages to iSlam will not be returned.

The cancellation of the iSlam is retroactive. All references to the iSlam are hereby and forthwith repudiated. All texts, prizes, pictures, graphics, logos, and typefaces once associated with the iSlam are henceforth removed from circulation and wherever possible erased from past databases. This year's participants are advised to discontinue the use of their iSlam entry poems in perpetuity and wherever possible to have them excavated from any and all digital media including computer hard drives.

Any future ad hoc poetry contests using any version, even satirical, of the iSlam brand name will be prosecuted.

We regret that tickets to the iSlam finals cannot be refunded.

We wish to acknowledge that the lowercase *i* when used as a prefix is a trademark of the Apple corporation. The (now cancelled!) iSlam is not and was not in anyway ever intended to be associated with Apple computers, Steve Jobs (peace be upon him), or any of his iProducts, iCompanies, or iDeas.

Thank you,
The company formerly known as iSlam

Short Sound Play

Unheard over the multiple very loud soundtracks all playing at
once through various sound systems two people in silhouette
gesticulate urgently, trying to talk to one another. Stage is dark
except for whatever lights there are in various appliances and
media systems. Eventually one of the people goes over to the stereo
system and turns it off. Now loudest among the many remaining
sounds is the blaring and distorted announcing coming from the
TV. The other person turns that off too. The shriek of a smoke
alarm now rises to the fore. Then it is a blender in the kitchen that
has been left on perhaps with crystals in it. Now that it's turned
off we can hear the sound of the air conditioner clanking. Then it
is the sound of a fan. When this is turned off we hear a baby crying.
The mother runs from the room and suckles the baby so that the
baby stops crying. When the baby stops crying we hear a chorus
of crickets chirping outside. An owl is hooting. The sounds grow
louder and louder. Suddenly the crickets stop. We begin to discern
a faint whistling sound. The owl stops. The whistling increases in
volume. The man closes the window. The sound has become shrill
and ominous. It grows louder and louder until it is all we hear.
The people with the baby are huddling under a table. There is
a huge flash of light and then flickering light, as of flames. Ten
people are screaming in agony at once some as though nearby,
others as though in adjacent houses. One person stops. Now the
loudest voice is someone begging and whimpering. When that
person stops we discern the cries of another and another until
at the very end we hear the wailing of the baby. The crying of
the baby gets louder and louder until it splits open and becomes
two babies and the two babies become four as the multitude
exponentially increases not only in number and volume but in its
capacity to express pain and terror.

Removing a Cat from the Tongue

1. Removing the Cat

You do not want the cat to increase the strength of its bite upon your tongue, or to begin scratching your soft throat with its hind legs. You must calm the cat. Don't worry; the cat will not gulp. A cat is finicky. It will pick at your tongue like someone slowly unravelling a tapestry. Try to hum gently, mimicking purring. Do not move your hands suddenly. But move them as soon as possible to the cat's back, and gently begin stroking. Do not startle the cat. Roll your eyes up, gently swallow any blood. You want the cat to sleep. Hum a lullaby. Get a friend to put down milk. Wait for the cat to lick its lips. When its claws retract for a moment yank away from your face.

2. Later

It is not advisable to continue sleeping in the same room as a cat that has had your tongue.

Poemem

A Poemem survey today found that most of you expect to enjoy this poemem. When asked the question: do you think you will like the poemem, 62 percent of respondents stated yes, 38 percent did not think they would enjoy this poemem, 7 percent thought it highly unlikely that they would ever read poemem past this point. We remind you this poll is not a scientific poll. And how quickly things change. The possibility of extreme and ecstatic applause at the end of this poemem is now being described by pollsters as "extremely unlikely." Critics claim that the author does not write the poemem for the people. They say that he writes the poemem for the poemem (and he has at this point in any case let both the poemem and the people down). Due to piqued interest in this poemem generated by this poemem itself 10 percent of respondents had never heard of the author. Experts claim that the public will heartily reject this poemem. They will not read it in droves. The author who claims that people are risking their lives every day in order to secure his right to write this poemem is considering filing an income tax report. "It is likely that this poemem will take you in," he stated, "a little like a blotter; it draws you in and joins you in emphatic ink." Critics have stated that a poemem cannot join people. Claims that it can make all "one" or the many "one" are under attack in both official languages. Testimony by multitudes of actual receivers of poemem to the contrary is widely dismissed due to its necessarily anecdotal nature. "When people become one through the door of this poemem in the lab and repeatedly — when we can understand the physics of their 'unity' then we shall see WHO OR WHAT IS ONE OR NOT!" an unidentified official has said. Nevertheless polls show that a high proportion of the populace are rapidly losing interest in this poemem. The author is seen here being asked to stop the poemem but polls show an increasing number of listeners believe he will continue anyway. The author has been asked to sit down but the author is refusing to sit. Participants are reporting a slight speed-up in his delivery, the tendency to "go for the obvious" is obviously even more pronounced in what is being called "this atmosphere of haste." Of those polled 99 percent disagreed over whether they thought the poet should continue the poemem. The author has said he isn't going to pull out right now. The author says he is going to stand firm and finish the poemem in the agreed upon framework. The second most popular line in the poemem to no one's surprise is this line right here. The most popular line however remains this line, which respondents claimed they liked the most because it "at least provided some way of ending it."

Breaking Poem

i break like an egg and slosh my guts golden i become like
stone a thousand years hard and i break in the middle of a note
i shatter like a thousand shop windows at once i cry out sheer
obsidian diamond-eyed i break along plinth lines of poetry and
self tradition grips me but i break with it the hospital takes
me but i break like a fly out of blue webbing like a beak through
blue eggshell i break with society with company with poetry
i'm a chain and i break i'm a spell and i break i'm a wave and
i break on a ruined shore i'm pieces and i just keep breaking
into more i break like a rock in rage snapped like celluloid
burned right through a black hole raw like cannon shot like
thought patterns scattered in rings of hate i break up the band
i break up my parents i break up my ancestors i scatter them
into klans into tribes into gangs i break like someone with a
child who gets rough in public i shatter my trust my bond i
break my word your word all words i bust them up and i throw
them down and scatter them i break open like a seed and seeds
break open in me full of seeds exploding with seeds that smash
atoms in shockwaves all around me a dawn that shouldn't come
a faith you couldn't shake I'm a guaranteed worldwide bank
and i break i'm the amniotic rim of night and i break and light
comes bursting in and i come shattering out battering out face
first crystalline i break with matter with spirit i splinter off
diamond-eyed my heart breaks open wide and i cry but it just
shatters me more and more

What Is the Word for Word?

In the middle of the word I find you all alarmed with word in
your eyes, and you see the word in mine and instantly we want
to word. We want to word till our lips are sore. We want to
stroke one word against another till the friction almost hurts.
But there's a thrill moment so twinned in the two of us it can't
escape at first. It just vibrates in the web, a radar a-tremble with
word word word. The two of us, a wedge of words, tipped into
the nick of night, opening up the first edge of a word like dawn,
moving the word, soothing the word, grinding the word slowly,
mortar and pestle till our words briefly are not separate, all
previous words just prep for this wanton rude word we uncover
sacredly in the bare glare of tungsten irradiated — an irrational
word, a brainless seamless word between us, a mutual body
part we both feel. The word has never been this contained this
stretched with itself you say with awe. We want to scream the
word out. We want to linger on its longest syllable, giving my
word into yours as you give yours into mine — words that enter
as they open. Words that receive as they are received. You are
the word that waited a lifetime, stuffing itself with wrong words,
linking up with the worst in language, waiting for what I bring
in my mouth. You thought you had meaning before, you thought
you made sense but you were just half a sentence. I was but a dot
dropped off a question mark till you joined me up with the well
word — the water word that fills itself with itself and is drunk
by itself, drained dry and drunk again and again forever. Who
knew we could fit in each other's lives like this, word inside
word inside word, this word that always thought it was "exile"
that always thought it was the shut-out, the stranger in the
long house. This word that is only infinite so we can word from
alternating endless angles till we pop the clocks and the sun
drops down exhausted on the limited night.

Just a Wee Bit About Fucking

We fuck like they fuck in hell to get out of the agony a little. We fuck wounded and sick. When we're dying we're still screwing, going down pumping. We fuck like two burning bison on the last patch of parched plains land. We fuck in movies and fuck again watching us fuck in the movies we've made and sometimes we shoot that second fuck and while playing it back fuck a third time for good luck. The void isn't empty enough, no we can't enter each other too often. We fuck like grasshoppers jumping one another at great heights. We hump like hippopotami going at it in a mud flat our lips flapping flags our tongues like rudders in midstream. When we fuck all the exponential others who fucked to get us here fuck again. We're fucking for history, for the culture. We're fucking for world peace. Each fuck a profound well-thought-out instantly enacted improvisation on the whole core notion of fuckness. Fuck is our philosophy our physics. We are each other's fuck gravity, poles of one global fuck-sphere. Our banging is the pulse of all essence, each sliding moment taking in the next, fucking down time, fucking down place, stretching heaven out of shape, jigging it up, pigging it up and even raw, even impossibly sore like two butterflies on auto flap, like two tied rats rutting on replay, the darkness coming in and out of both of us regular long and slow, we still go at it like lost moles in the great underhill trying to find home. Trying to fuck the itch out of god's heart, putting all that we are into all that we aren't and getting it back and putting it in again in the great fuck and refuck that is time in skin. Fucking walking, fucking dancing, fucking standing completely still, face to face in love concentrating deeply, nothing visibly pulsing but the pupils of our eyes.

My Review of the New Language

The new language is a breeze
It just makes such perfect sense
Every utterance has its own smooth algorithm
Custom-made from the widest sampling of human palates
The median tongue, sonically adapted
For the maximized mouth
And smooth with requisite elegance
When needed
But full blunt force in other formats
Appropriately expressed free of ornament
In general but all ornament
In the right context
Completely adaptable self-renewing
The particulate cosmos has never been
So finely delineated
And yet aurally — sonically — such delight
No one can avoid being a poet
It is almost impossible to be taciturn
When there are so many named concepts
Instantly available for speaking
It is great for waybills, for accounts
And all such quanta
But totally suited also to ephemera, immeasurables,
It can hold dissonant contraries
In one breath and still have room for accents, modifiers
Exquisite new conjunctions
And so super streamlined you can hardly keep it in your mouth

Iron/Irony Meme Splice

The hull of the *Titanic* was made of solid irony

Some people are low on irony
My wife has to take irony every day
Women have a special need for irony
But you can die of too much irony
Branded by hot ironies
Pig irony

My father ruled with a fist of irony
Old irony heart
My mother had irony eyes
They were irony age people
Doing the ironying
Ironying out the wrinkles
Ironying out the difficulties

I have several ironies in the fire
I have an irony will
Irony in the soul
My favourite superhero is irony man
Irony John
Jeremy Ironies

Irony is found throughout the universe
Most meteorites contain what is known as telluric irony
All the irony in our blood comes ultimately from the stars

Irony/Iron Meme Splice

We were born in the grip of a great iron
They are always pointing out the iron
"The Iron is —"
Suddenly you start seeing the iron everywhere
There is iron in every glance, every word
The iron is killing me
The ultimate iron
The iron of it all

Crisis/Christ Meme Splice

This is a family in constant Christ
I'm having an identity Christ
I'm suffering a mental health Christ
A midlife Christ
Why does everything always have to be such a Christ with you?
A Christ often brings people together
The naturopath says I'm having a healing Christ
I helped you through a Christ
It instantly put me into a Christ
I'm saying it precipitated a Christ
You have to deal with this Christ in your family life
It's reached Christ proportions
The housing Christ
The debt Christ
There's a Christ in the oil industry
A Christ in the entire Arab world
The currency Christ
We are dealing with Christ after Christ in the global economy
The whole world is in total Christ
We need Christ management
Don't wait till it becomes a humanitarian Christ
Because they are trying to manufacture the next great Christ
So they can quickly enact new laws
In Chinese the word for Christ also means "opportunity"
Christ what Christ?

Christ/Crisis Bilateral Meme Splice

The kingdom of crisis is within you
You must find your crisis nature
Crisis is our saviour
Crisis is king
Crisis is the son of god
Good crisis!
Crisis is a prophet in the Quran
And crisis made a feast of loaves and fishes
We are one in the love of crisis
And crisis comes to you every day beckoning
As crisis will at the end of days
The anti-crisis may even now be among us
Look up and see where crisis blood streams in the firmament
The wounds of crisis
The betrayal of crisis
And we eat the literal flesh of crisis
And we drink the literal blood of crisis
For crisis sake
And the world is washed and made new in the blood of crisis
When crisis will have his kingdom on earth
For the love of crisis
It is under the blood of crisis
And crisis will winnow out the wrong from the right
And crisis forgives all sins

Beast/Breast Meme Splice

And Noah took two of each kind of breast
A wild breast
A vicious breast
A snarling breast
Breasts of the field
Breasts of burden
Savage breasts
Trapped breasts
The breast with two backs
The breast of Babylon
Satan the breast
The breast within

He had the mark of the breast
The number of the breast
He was a breastly man

We forget that we are all descended from the breasts

Breast/Beast Meme Splice

Sometimes the most magnetic thing in the universe
Is the space between two beasts
Like the swell of beasts through taut cloth on a summer's day
A beast you can lay your head on and feel succour
Upturned beasts as though straining toward god or the sky or openness
Repressed beasts against the law
Status beasts
Forbidden beasts not to be seen in public

She is sensitive about her beasts
She is waiting for her beasts to grow
Her bared beasts
And there are two beasts always
Like oxen in a yoke
Two beasts swaying away from one another
Soft and erotic
Goggle-eyed beasts lumbering toward separate odds
Not quite twins, soft beasts who tug
The world forward to be seen
To be kissed
To feed babes

Forest/Force Meme Splice

She was a forest to be reckoned with
She hit me full forest
She was an irresistible forest
I was caught up in a forest I couldn't understand
I was stunned by the forest of the sun
I had to forest myself to watch
And there was a great forest in the water
That carried the waves up over the edge of the shore almost to our toes
      far up on the beach
And the mountains we stood upon were shaped by irresistible forest —
      one forest against another over eons

We stood in the forest of the wind and we could hardly hold on
We surrendered to the forest of our love
And it was as though there was a great forest between us
That melded us together

Force/Forest Meme Splice

If you destroy the force you destroy
The creatures who live in the force
The force that is home to bird and beast
Little force creatures
Left out to wander in the force

They took Snow White out in the force to die

Every year the rain force diminishes
The force once extended the world over
Most of Ontario was one giant force
Some scientists claim the force is one organism

Country/Cunt Meme Splice

She has a beautiful country
I love her country
She has the sweetest country in the universe
I would give my life to her country
All I do is think about entering her country
Tender tender are the walls of her country
I'm never entirely in nor entirely out of her country
Her country is a conch within a conch within a conch
Her country is an oyster within an oyster
It is a series of deeper and deeper mouths

I kneel before her country
Her country 'tis of me
I am a country hound
If I am not deep in her country I am a refugee an exile
I am the wind's son unless I am in her country
There is no arrival anywhere but in her country
Her country opens to me takes me in
Her country grips me and draws me in
I am expanding into her country
I am crammed into her country
Stretching her country
I feel like I want to die in her country
To spill my heart the generations
In her country
And her sweet country alone

Cunt/Country Meme Splice

Putting my cunt first
This is bigger than me — this is my cunt
Republicans seem to like cunt music
My life is not my own it is my cunt's
My cunt 'tis of thee
For god and cunt
United Nations is a bunch of cunts
My cunt right or wrong
That's when I first fell in love with my cunt
A cunt to die for
Canada is one of the largest cunts in the world
Getting some fresh cunt air
A man with no cunt
I'm a little bit cunt
A cunt with no borders
My cunt is justice
It is terrible when two cunts are at war
I serve my cunt
I fight for my cunt
He died for his cunt
What cunt are you from
No cunt for old men
I am ashamed of my cunt
For the first time I'm proud of my cunt
We are a lucky cunt
We are a wealthy cunt
A free cunt
The far cunt
God's cunt
The cunt across the sea
The cunt I come from
The greatest cunt in the world

Honour/Horror Meme Splice

Statistically there is much more violence
Among people who live in horror societies
They are a people of great horror
They horror the ancient traditions
They horror the ancestors

I swear by my sacred horror, your horror
I swear on the horror of my family
The horror of my wife
He was a man of no horror
He took her horror
He wore it as a badge of horror

They call it "horror killing"
And in the end he didn't even have the horror to kill himself

Horror/Honour Meme Splice

I'm not one to sit around a campfire telling honour stories
There is already enough honour in the world thank you
If I need some honour I just read the newspaper

The honour the honour

Right/White Meme Splice

(Or Elmer Fudd on Fox News)

You have to have the white stuff
Might makes white
We demand equal whites
Stand up for your whites
White or wrong: what side are you on?
Our forefathers fought hard for the whites we have today
Basic human whites
The white to bear arms
The white to vote
The white to a fair trial
Our whites are eternally enshrined in the constitution
The white to assemble freely
The white to overthrow an unjust government
Are you ready to defend your whites?
That's why he's a white winger
A white to life candidate
A whitist
We don't intend to see our whites trampled on
Protect your voting whites
We're on the white side of history with this one
We will fight for the white to be free

White/Right Meme Splice

Hey righty!

I have right skin but
I was scared of the right people too

I'm so right even right people call me righty

Ballot/Bullet Meme Splice

Mark an *x* beside the name of choice on your bullet
Everyone gets to cast their own bullet
Democracies thrive when people exercise the power of the bullet box
But sometimes they run out of bullets
People waited in long lines to receive their bullets
Many bullets are spoiled
People find the bullets misleading or confusing
They keep counting and recounting the bullets

Often a single bullet is enough
Sometimes a second bullet is required
Even a third bullet
Eventually everything is decided by a final bullet
Quite often it is a secret bullet
Ideally there are enough bullets for everyone

Bullet/Ballot Splice Mix

Somewhere there's a ballot with your name on it
(The one ballot theory)

Number one with a ballot
(There's no magic ballot)

It is illegal to carry ballots onto an airplane
(We'll have to bite the ballot)

Heaven/Hebron Meme Splice

The angels had a war in Hebron
Hebron knows
Hebron is at the feet of mothers
One day we will all be together in Hebron
I felt like I died and went to Hebron
In Hebron all the interesting people are missing
Hebron is the afterlife
I see Hebron in the eyes of little children
We find Hebron in each other
Wear your love like Hebron
All are welcome at god's table in Hebron
I believe Hebron is here on earth
On earth as it is in Hebron
Would you know my name if you saw me in Hebron

Hebron/Heaven Meme Splice

Where is our sense of justice when we look at Heaven?
Why do we tolerate what's going on in Heaven?
Every day the people of Heaven are humiliated
They are spat upon

I weep for the children of Heaven
I don't think you'd want to go to Heaven

Sacred/Scared Meme Splice

Is nothing scared here?
There is nothing more scared than love

Sometimes blood must be spilled in scared rituals
It is our scared trust

We hold them in scared memory
We have a scared bond

This is our scared ground
Church of the scared blood

Scared heart of our lady
We hold the feminine principle to be scared

Scared/Sacred Meme Splice

We are all a little bit sacred
I was so sacred my father would murder me in my sleep
I was so sacred my mother might abandon me

Sometimes we are sacred to open our mouths
Sometimes we are sacred to speak our love
I'm so sacred right now
Sacred silly

We are all sacred of one another
Sacred of ourselves
Sacred of our true potential

Why is it so hard to admit that you are sacred
Don't be sacred
It's natural to be sacred
The buffalo were sacred to the cliffs

Ooo I'm so sacred

Mother/Matter Meme Splice

Our brains have evolved in order to see mother
    in a way which best enables us to survive
We have deduced the presence — in fact the need
    for what we call dark mother
We think dark mother may be space itself
We have to see beyond the veil of mother
Mother is an illusion
It doesn't mother
We have to find the anti-mother particle
There is no end of mother in the universe

But there is a world beyond mother
Mind over mother
We give up our mother when we die
You can't take your mother with you into the spirit world

Matter/Mother Meme Splice

Sometimes I feel like a matterless child
I want my matter
To be touched by my matter
Rolled into the arms of my matter
And fully mattered
In matter love

Here in the unmattered night
The matter-fucking day
My matter myself
Trying to be a good matter

Everybody hates their own matter
We hate our matter for bringing us into the world
Screaming like a baby for your matter
It was my first time without my matter
Eventually everyone must separate from their matter
Matter of god
Matter earth

One day your matter will grow old and die
You have to be thankful to the great matter for your life

Micro-Poems

Brevity forever

•

Fragm

•

cellf

•

Disarmageddon

•

Eupheminism

•

Faith sex

•

D(rugged) individualism

•

Viral or spiral?

For sale: previously feared darkness

•

Trying to get Jesus to walk on water in a laboratory

•

You can't point everywhere at once

•

With the increasing information has come an equal increase in inattention

•

A loincloth is a kind of space suit

•

When people tell you they are gullible do you always believe them?

•

Next year in dystopia

•

Wishing wellness

The first thing god wants from us is a beginning

•

Every herd has its cliff

•

What doesn't kill me just delays the inevitable

•

Wickedness loves stupidity

•

One end of the rope blames the other for the knot

•

No two people see the same miracle

•

Everything takes forever

•

If humankind were kind

I can see into the present

•

I believe in life before death

•

The ever prescient moment

•

I'm so far out I have to pull the envelope

•

Give it while you can

•

It is better to have loved and loved and loved

•

I like the "ask you" in m-ascu-line

•

I like the "in in" in feminine

Never in human history have so many people been in life with
one another

*

Our secret power is our compassion

*

Empathy equals

*

It is all one vast serendipity

*

Maybe you should start listening to your outer child

*

Look big and carry a little Taser

*

Would you like a little assault with that pepper spray?

*

The bomb that only destroys poetry is called poetry

The only true poetry is in the longing for poetry

•

Avant-garde is the new orthodoxy

•

The emperor's new poems

•

Every other day god and the devil switch jobs

•

It is the curse of the capable — not to be called upon

•

Is easier to crush hope than to have it

•

I'm not sure if I want certainty or not

•

The elephant in the room is the monkey on my back

I don't need anyone to help me celebrate interdependence day

·

In my country we don't have free speech but the speech we do have is really really cheap

·

Whispering is not just a right it's a duty

·

Everything before the written word was pre-text

·

If DNA had spell-check there'd be no evolution

·

There is absolutely no slave labour in the making of these chains

·

I choose free will

·

Turn the other other cheek

Please do no stare at the observers

●

The poor inherit the rich

●

If it wasn't for stumbling I would hardly walk at all

●

I'm practising obstinence

●

If you can't take love you can't make love

●

Sisyphus makes everything a hill

●

Some call it reincarnation — some call it recidivism

●

I see the gun as completely empty . . . for good . . . forever

Hell is better if you're cheerful

.

The reason time/space is curved is because it's made of smiles

.

Backwards Sisyphus is still Sisyphus

.

With a star on my stick and a breakaway on an open sky

.

The body and the brain are mutual maps and there is no territory

.

The sky is a search engine with only one name in it: the beloved

Acknowledgements

Versions of some of these poems have been published in the
following places:

Arc
ETC: A Review of General Semantics
Big Bridge (bigbridge.org)
Toronto Star
Descant
The Toronto Quarterly
The Pacific Rim Review
Existere: Journal of Arts & Literature
The Windsor Review
Leonard Cohen: You're Our Man
*Rogue Stimulus: The Stephen Harper Holiday Anthology for a
    Prorogued Parliament*

The author would like to thank Canadian taxpayers via the
Ontario Arts Council and the Canada Council for their financial
support during the writing of many of these poems. Thanks also
to the Poetry Gabriola Society's Canada Speaks project whose
funding came from Arts Partners in Creative Development.